3 Fundamental Principles of Sophro-ki® Sophrology

DORNA REVIE

DEDICATION

To the person who recommended that I take Sophrology sessions in 1989, when I was in Burn Out. Little did I know how much that little decision would change my life..

CONTENTS

ACKNOWLEDGMENTS

To all my great Sophro-ki® Sophrology team without whom this
first book would not exist..

WHAT IS SOPHRO-KI® SOPHROLOGY?

"Stop anxiety, worry, sleep problems, stress, overwhelm, and. confidently take charge of your own life."

"Sophro-ki® Sophrology took me from Burn Out to feeling stronger and more at ease in the world than ever before. As I continue to practice, I keep wondering how my life could be even better than it is now? And then I find out!"

Dorna Revie
Founder and CEO
Energy Centre Sarl and Sophro-ki® Sophrology Center Online

Sophro-ki® Sophrology is an organic way of bringing your life together, discovering how to harness and fully express your inner strengths and motivations, and moving forward with confidence, trust and inner happiness.

Fast becoming the **technique of choice** for the hectic, action packed lifestyles, it is easy to include in a busy schedule.

The 5min - 20min exercises can easily be done anywhere, anytime, without the need or distraction of added external influences like music, candles, essential oils and without special clothes, mats, quiet places or meditation and fitness aids.

It is a grass-roots approach – just you and your body.

The beauty of Sophro-ki® Sophrology lies in its simplicity and adaptability, combined with the level of depth at which one can choose to practise it.

It is inspired from Yoga, Buddhism and Zen, and incorporates elements of visualisation, meditation, mindfulness, breathing and simple movements for relaxation all brought together to create structured sets of exercises.

"The key is simply to keep noticing and discovering the physical sensations."

Imagine…

Freeing yourself from your 'normal' problems and worries

Doing away with anxiety and negativity,

Waking up each morning **feeling fully alive,** ready to enjoy life?

Sophro-ki® Sophrology exercises guide us to be as much as possible in present time. **In the NOW.**

Gradually, this allows the mind to become clearer, more focused and also more spacious and the body to relax and balance.

"To be anxious, worried or scared the mind needs to be in the past or the future."

To be able to be anxious, worried or scared we need to be thinking about the past or the future.

When we are fully present we are in action, just doing what needs to be done right now in this moment of time.

For example: If a huge tiger jumped into the room just now you would immediately run for the door, get out and slam it shut. Then you start to shake and tremble from the shock.

Afterwards you start to think about what to do next (going into the future) and are 'anxious' to find a solution. Once you have found somebody to take the tiger away, you tell your friends, go over the story, think how lucky you were and possibly also imagine what could have happened if you had not made the door in time.

You may not manage to sleep for a while because you are imagining what might have happened.

The actions are in the present time, the body and mind are focused and reacting to the surroundings. The after reflections and projections are what makes anxiety, fear, and worry These are habits we have learned that can be useful for future decisions but are not useful if they become chronic and contaminate daily life.

"Sophro-ki® Sophrology Level one is all about training the mind into present time."

We do this with The Body Scan – noticing each part of the body without judging or without trying to alter it in any way. The body is always in present time and so focusing on the body brings the mind into present time too.

Really quite simple to know but regular practice is required to make it a way of life...

WHAT ARE THE ORIGINS?

Professor Alfonso Caycedo, Neuropsychiatrist, doing his medical studies in Spain after the civil war, originally set out to find a way of improving the lives of depressed and war traumatised patients with **minimal use of drugs and psychiatric treatments.**

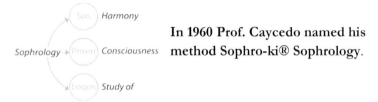

In 1960 Prof. Caycedo named his method Sophro-ki® Sophrology.

The word 'Sophro-ki® Sophrology' comes from the Greek

Sos- harmony'

Phren – Consciousness

Logos – Study of

Sophro-ki® Sophrology translated from Greek means:

"The Study of Consciousness in Harmony"

In practical terms each Sophro-ki® Sophrology exercise guides us to discover more and more about how our body, mind, emotions and values operate thus leading to expansion of our self-knowledge and eventually to living in full consciousness. We gradually create our own personal 'How life works - Operational Manual!'

4

Sophro-ki® Sophrology brings together Eastern Philosophies and Western science. It is inspired by yoga, Buddhism and Zen, as well as phenomenology, cognitive psychology and autogenic training and more.

In the 1950s when Sophro-ki® Sophrology was created, the main psychology method used by psychologists was psycho-analysis. This meant that people were invited to go back to the past to find the cause of what was wrong in their present life.

Professor Caycedo, through his experience and studies of applied phenomenology and through his marriage to a yoga teacher, his research into Eastern disciplines and philosophies, realised the immense benefits of bringing the mind into present time.

Sophro-ki® Sophrology is a structured tried and tested method developed from more than 50 years of experience and documented results.

Over the years, Prof. Caycedo along with help from Dr. Raymond Abrezol and many other Sophro-ki® Sophrology teachers, updated and improved the Sophro-ki® Sophrology method.

Prof. Caycedo was a visionary who realized that a stress reduction method that could be easily applied and had long term results was going to be essential in the fast paced world of the future.

Sophro-ki® Sophrology started as a 4 step transformational process and has now developed into an extensive method of Three Cycles and 12 levels.

Each cycle contains 4 levels. Typically it takes at least 3 years to complete the three cycles.

Plus the continuing use and repetition of the exercises help us to continue our self-development for the rest of our lives.

As we repeat the exercises we uncover and discover more parts of our own personal Operational Manual and life becomes easier and easier and more and more enjoyable.

"As we repeat the exercises we continually uncover and discover more parts of our own personal Operational Manual and life becomes easier and easier and more and more enjoyable."

For many years, there were only the first four levels and typically these four are the ones taught in most Sophro-ki® Sophrology schools.

Now it is possible to go deeper into Sophro-ki® Sophrology and complete 3 cycles, making twelve levels in total. The learnings and discoveries from the first four levels will be all that most people require in order to discover, develop and transform their daily lives.

"The learnings and discoveries from the first four levels will be all that most people require in order to discover, develop and transform their daily lives."

As you make your way through the levels it is as if you are shining a light onto various aspects of your life and bringing to light aspects of yourself and the world around you. You can then decide whether you want to keep those parts as they are or transform them.

We start with The Reductive Cycle which is made up of the first four levels of Sophro-ki® Sophrology.

Typically in group sessions you would expect to do from six to ten sessions for each level, however, as an individual Sophro One-2-One client, the process is tailor-made and you may spend longer or shorter with each of the levels depending on your needs and goals.

WHAT IS THE PROCESS?

There are 3 cycles of Sophro-ki® Sophrology and within each cycle there are 4 levels (12 levels in total)

1st cycle - The Reductive Cycle

Reductive comes from phenomenology. Putting aside all that you think you know and believe and looking at the world through new eyes. Seeing everything 'as if it is the first time'.

Learning to observe what is actually there, what is actually happening instead of looking through the filters of our inner programming.

In the first cycle there are four levels each with its own focus and theme that guide us to become more aware and to live more consciously.

LEVEL ONE

In the First Level, you will be guided to notice physical sensations in your body that you have never noticed before.

You will discover how you can be happy right now and also how to experience and nurture inner happiness.

In our society we tend to only notice the body when it is hurting or sick. In Sophro-ki® Sophrology we start to notice the different parts of the body when they are healthy.

Just doing this simple exercise makes a big difference to daily life.

"Level 1 is about being happy right now."

Inspired from Raja Yoga there are very simple relaxation exercises to help us to become more aware of the body and increase present time awareness.

You can expect improvements in concentration, self-confidence and the amount of smiling.

Reduction in anxiety, worry, stress and stress related problems such as sleep, digestion, back pain etc…

You are encouraged to live in the present, without judgment and to experience the world as if seeing it 'for the first time'

LEVEL TWO

In the Second Level, you will learn to explore your 5 senses and what happens when your mind interprets these through the filters of the beliefs and attitudes that you have learned over the years.

You will then be able to decide whether these attitudes and beliefs are still useful or not.

If not you will learn how to change them. In this level we become aware of all the happy and enjoyable events waiting for us in the future.

Typically, people feel even more in control. You learn to restart to be the observer and are less caught up in situations giving you more space to evaluate and make better choices and decisions.

Inspired from Buddhism we become aware of the workings of the mind and discover the power of thoughts, words and the inner senses.

"Level 2 is about realising that the future could also bring happiness."

Reduction in mind chatter, unpleasant thought patterns and fear of the future.

The exercises are designed to create a positive outlook, focusing on goals, projects, and future events.

LEVEL THREE

In the Third Level, you will focus on emotions and notice how they link the mind and body together.

You will learn about managing your emotions and also increasing impact of the ones that you like best and diminishing impact the ones that you prefer not to have.

Each emotion is there for a reason and we also learn how to interpret our emotions and appreciate them.

In this level we also go into the past to search for those happy, positive moments that we remember and also many that we have forgotten.

Even if life has not been good to us we have ways of finding even tiny little moments of kindness and joy. Remembering and acknowledging these moments builds a strong foundation of confidence, love and trust.

Typically, people find that they can more easily manage their emotions, have a greater sense of security, stronger foundations and more support from the world around them.

Based on Zen. We now start walking mediation where, with, eyes partly open become more aware of the world around us and that we are capable of moving through time and space.

"Level 3 is about reinforcing foundations by rediscovering supportive times in the past."

The main focus areas: The emotions, reduction in unpleasant memories, and feelings like anger, guilt, shame, and not being good enough.

LEVEL FOUR

In the fourth level, we explore our personal values, society's values and existential values.

We do this by personally experiencing them and noticing how these values play out in our own life and how they affect each tiny decision that we make during each day.

We also do walking meditations in which we experience the oneness of life and our connectedness to all.

The concept of time and space as living reality.

Typically, after this level people discover that the life that they dreamed of at the beginning of the first level is now in place and they are actually living it.

We go through the checklist of their wishes and tick them off as being completed. If there are still some that have not yet materialized they are now competent and experienced enough to know what to do and how to get there.

"Level 4 is based on the experience and research gathered from the first 3 levels. We experience 'All is One' and explore values."

Transformation – Life can be perceived in many different ways, the world shows up differently, deep inner knowing that all is well, deep inner confidence, knowing who you are, intuitive awareness.

There is also a huge reduction in doubts about who you are, if you are doing the right thing, if you are good enough and other unhelpful judgments.

The main focus areas: Personal values, the dimensions of time and space, the personal experience of yourself as a valued human being.

The main Sophro-ki® Sophrology values are: Dignity, Freedom and Responsibility

These four levels make up the Foundation Cycle in Sophro-ki® Sophrology and as I mentioned earlier were the only ones available for many years and are typically the ones that most people will do and be completely satisfied with.

If, however, when you finish the First Cycle and you feel inclined to go more deeply into the self-discovery process then you can continue your journey of exploration on into the Second and Third Cycles.

2nd cycle - The Radical Cycle

Radical meaning – back to the roots. There are Four Levels in this cycle. Radical means going back to basics, to the source. The source of who we are.

We now learn awareness of ourselves in time and space between the infinitely small and the infinitely large. We ask contemplate questions like 'Who am I?' How can I know myself?

Using our voice to vibrate our cells, molecules and atoms we start exploring the beginning of life, the universe and the beginning of time. Each person will have their own personal experience of these concepts and nobody is right or wrong.

Whatever shows up and whatever the experience we accept it and observe it in a phenomenological way.

That is: without judgment, as if it is the first time. With an open mind and with curiosity and wonder. Each person's experience is interesting, thought provoking and leads us to contemplate these topics and to experience our daily life from different perspectives.

This may all seem very esoteric and mind orientated, however, the actual experiences are very real and very profound. Sophro-ki® Sophrology is, above all, a practical and experiential process.

"Each person will have their own personal experience of the exercise and nobody is right or wrong, however, the experiences are interesting, thought provoking and allow us to view and experience our daily life from different perspectives."

Having reinforced the mental and physical structures during the first cycle, you now go on to discover your place in the universe.

These levels are based on the concepts of the first four, however, you have now journeyed along the spiral of life and will now experience all four levels from a different view point and perception. During this level sound (the voice) is used to activate the body, mind and spirit.

Awareness of percussion of the voice vibrations in each of the cells leads to a deeper integration of consciousness.

3rd cycle - The Existential Cycle

The Third Cycle is called **The Existential Cycle. Existential meaning – exploring our existence and existential values**.

Using all the skills that we have learned and discoveries we have made during Cycles One and Two we explore relationships and the conscious interaction with the people and world around us.

We take note of what happens, what part we are playing and what changes if we alter tiny parts of our own framework and structure.

In the existential Cycle we notice how values and our intentionality direct our life, our relationships and our perceptions of the world.

The three main values of Sophro-ki® Sophrology training are Freedom, Responsibility and Dignity. We will explore these to discover what they mean to us and also to our interaction with others.

You not only continue to train to be fully present in each moment in time, but also to be aware of all the dimensions of space and time and to be fully in tune with yourself, the world around you and the universe.

There are also four levels in this Cycle based on the first and second cycles, however, again you have moved along the spiral of life and experience the exercises from a new and different perspective.

Sophro-ki® Sophrology training is about letting your own light shine. This final cycle is about fully integrating the whole program so that, as Marianne Williamson so rightly put, you inspire others to open themselves and allow their light to shine.

You have now learned to be very conscious of your thoughts, words and actions and can consciously fully love and appreciate the life you are living.

We will continue to use the vibrations of the vowels sounds that we vocalise as well as becoming fully aware of our personal values and how they affect every tiny decision that we take during the day.

Typically, after this level life just keeps on getting better and better.

I would like to point out though that experiencing life and perceiving life and being better and better does not mean that we are insulated from the ups and downs of life and from all the incidents, events and problems that happen to everybody else.

What happens is that the way we perceive this events makes them much more manageable and we are able to take away the lessons from them and put them in the past where they belong rather than ruminating on them and producing negative emotions.

After finishing the Three Cycles we then continue to choose an exercise each day and continue to learn more, discover more and make our way towards full consciousness.

WHY MIGHT WE WANT TO LIVE IN FULL CONSCIOUSNESS?

Becoming aware or conscious of something that we are doing, believing or experiencing that is not pleasant or is not leading us towards the results we would like, is the first step necessary to decide whether or not we want to change it.

Becoming aware or conscious of something that we are doing, believing or experiencing that is pleasant and is leading us towards the results we want then we can repeat this more often, do more of the same and produce even better and more consistent positive results.

So whether we would like increase the positive or 'feel good' or decrease the negative or 'feel not good' experiences we need to first discover or become conscious of what we are personally doing that is helping to produce these.

It is not only people with problems who benefit from Sophro-ki® Sophrology, but also people who are leading the highly successful fulfilling lives.

We can all benefit from becoming more conscious. When people have chronic anxiety, fear and worry the results are swift and effective, however, they often need a bit longer to turn things around and integrate these new learnings.

People who, on the other hand, are already thinking and acting in positive and constructive ways, on discovering in detail their personal success process, immediately start to consciously and creatively implement what they have learned and excitedly watch the results increase exponentially.

It is recommended to practise the levels in their proposed order to fully experience the benefits of each. However, since they programme is holistic each exercise contains seeds of the whole system producing development on all levels at the same time. We will talk about this later in 'The Principle of Positive Action.'

Over the years, Prof. Caycedo along with help from Dr. Raymond Abrezol and many other Sophro-ki® Sophrology teachers, updated and improved the Sophro-ki® Sophrology method. He realised that a stress reduction method that could be easily applied and had long term results was going to be essential in the fast paced world of the future.

The Sophro-ki® Sophrology method has now developed into the 12 levels which are now being taught and that are gaining in popularity worldwide.

Sophro-ki® Sophrology has been very popular for many decades in France, Belgium, Spain, Colombia, Japan, Korea and Switzerland.

The three fundamental principles of Sophro-ki® Sophrology are; to bring oneself into the present, to reinforce positive action and to develop an objective reality.

WHAT IS THE AIM OF SOPHRO-KI®
SOPHROLOGY?

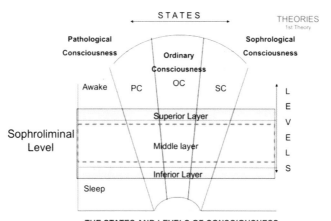

THE STATES AND LEVELS OF CONSCIOUSNESS

The aim of Sophro-ki® Sophrology is to teach people how to live in full consciousness. We call it sophrological consciousness in and in psychology it is generally known as super consciousness.

In the diagram above you can see the Sophro-ki® Sophrology diagram of the States and Levels of Consciousness. The levels go from up to down, from awake to the sophroliminal level and to then sleep.

The Sophro-ki® Sophrology exercises are done in the sophroliminal level which is the level of consciousness between awake and asleep.

The states of consciousness are from left to right.

Pathological consciousness: This is when we are sick with life threatening diseases and severe psychological problems on the far left to cold, flu, chronic anxiety and worry towards the right of this section.

Ordinary Consciousness: This is where most of us are most of the time. We are automatically going about our daily life and getting the jobs done, organizing, managing working. State of health okay.

Sophrological consciousness: is when we are fully in present time, living through our senses, fully experiencing each moment and getting the most out of each instant.
State of health, feeling of being fully alive, aware, present, oneness.

In a Sophro-ki® Sophrology exercise we start in the awake level and somewhere between pathological and sophrological state. The sophrologist guides us through the body scan, tension release and energizer. The mind calms down, the body relaxes and we find that we are now in the level between awake and asleep. It is in this level of consciousness that we do the specific Sophro-ki® Sophrology exercise.

This might be a gentle physical exercise or a mental exercise or both. The sophrologist then asks you to move and stretch the body and when you are ready to open your eyes. After we have done a Sophro-ki® Sophrology exercise we have moved more to the right of the diagram and are in or nearer the sophrological state of consciousness. More calm, more present and happier.

The three principles that of Sophro-ki® Sophrology are fundamental elements leading us to experiencing more and more often the state of sophrological consciousness.

WHAT ARE THE THREE PRINCIPLES?

NO. 1
BODY CONSCIOUSNESS

In Sophro-ki® Sophrology connecting with your body and becoming conscious of how it reacts to your thoughts and expresses emotions is one of the most important aspects.

Your body is often the only part of you that is actually in present time. In our society minds are usually in the past or in the future and rarely present to what is actually happening right now.

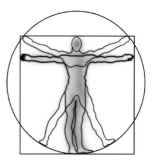

At the start of every Sophro-ki® Sophrology exercise we do a body scan in which you check in to see what is happening in your body. You are guided to notice all the physical sensation in each small part of your body.

These sensations are the proof that you are alive. In Sophro-ki® Sophrology we call these physical sensations 'vivances' or 'aliveness's'.

21

It is these 'aliveness's' that dictate our life.

They are what we consult before we make each decision and we continuously long for and search for happy, enjoyable aliveness's.

However, most of us have never been trained to notice them or to even think that they might be important and so we are mostly unconscious of them unless they are really strong or uncomfortable.

These aliveness's, however, play an important and constant role in our daily life. When we walk around a food market how do we decide what to buy? We decide whether we would like it or not.

How do we know if we would like it or not? When we see the food we either have pleasant physical sensations in the body (usually associated with liking) or unpleasant sensations (usually associated with disliking). We just take this for granted and don't usually think about how we know or don't know we just do it.

When we go to buy a car, a house, clothes, furniture, anything in fact, we tend to choose what we think will make us happy – how do we know it will make us happy? We have what we name 'happy sensations' in the body.

Sometimes, of course, we make a mistake. How do we know that we made a mistake? What we thought would give us happy physical sensations, actually, when we got home and experienced it, we felt physical sensations of sad, angry, or frustrated.

Basically physical sensation are all there is. We are constantly wanting, trying, finding ways to escape from unpleasant ones produce more pleasant ones.

So simply by becoming aware of our physical body sensations and learning to activate the ones we like best whenever we would like to feel them, without any outside stimulus is, in fact, the key to deep inner happiness.

We can then let go of 'needing', 'having', 'wanting', and just enjoy being.

One of the first exercises that we do in Sophro-ki® Sophrology is called 'Mood Lifting'. Towards the end of this exercise the client is asked to think of a moment of happiness that they experienced either yesterday or today. Something very simple like the sun shining, somebody smiling, listening to some lovely music, eating some nice food, etc.

They are then asked to experience this happy moment as if it is happening right now using as many of their senses as possible, smell, sounds, taste, touch, colour, shapes.

The client is then asked to notice the physical reactions within the body. Where in the body are you aware of this happiness? What physical sensations does happiness produce in your body?

Generally people say things like, warmth, lightness or tingling, however, if this exercise is done in a group each person will discover that they have slightly different physical sensations in slightly different places in their body than the others.

Next the client will be asked to let go of the happy moment memory and just enjoy the sensations of happiness within their body.

We do this three times in the exercise and the client can either choose the same happy moment or three different ones. It doesn't matter which they choose what matters is noticing what effect the happy moment memories have on the body.

Once they have discovered how their body lets them know that it is happy then they can choose to activate happiness whenever they want to feel happy.

The more they practice this exercise the happier they feel. Since most of us want to be happy and spend much time and money to produce this happy feeling, we can save a lot of time and money but just activating happiness within the body.

Experiencing this shift from the thinking mind to focusing on the physical body can be quite surprising for many people. After all we do not spend a lot of time consciously noticing the body unless there is pain. What we are asking you to do is to notice the body when it is joyful and happy.

We can also do a similar Sophro-ki® Sophrology exercise in which we experience love, being in love and being loved. After practicing for a while we will be able to feel love and loved whenever we choose to. Body consciousness meaning awareness of 'aliveness's' provides us with a broad band of information that is normally only experienced subconsciously. As we become more practiced in the art of noticing the body our intuition improves.

Regularly focusing on the body, and just observing and experiencing it without judging it or wanting it to be different is an ancient Buddhist meditation technique that calms the mind and also brings in more energy into the body.

The importance of body consciousness is fundamental to personal growth, the health of the mind and the body. It is allows us to experience true freedom choice, manage ourselves and become fully responsible for our lives.

NO. 2
POSITIVE ACTION

In Sophro-ki® Sophrology practice we learn to focus on what makes us feel good. We practice discovering, experiencing and living the physical sensations of happiness in the body.

By regularly practising focusing on the 'feel good' elements we set in motion a general trend that leads to a more positive attitude to life.

The principle of positive action is that when we think of something happy the body also expresses happiness. We are a holistic system and so whenever one tiny thing changes it has repercussions on the whole system.

It is now known that brain cells that fire together wire together and therefore, by continually focusing on and repeatedly remembering what made us feel good, the nice things people have said to us, the great music we listened to, the delicious food we ate, etc., we create neural motorways that take us easily and free flowingly towards more 'feel good' experiences.

Positive thoughts and the intention to notice positive situations, and the enjoyment of physical sensations of happiness, start a positive chain-reaction inside ourselves.

Each positive action impacts positively on all aspects of our self and our lives.

We can start the positive action from the mind by remembering a happy moment or we can start a positive action with the body by doing something that makes us happy.

Either way the body and mind will interact, positive thoughts produce positive body reactions.

Positive body movements produce positive thoughts.

Sophro-ki® Sophrology practice of positive action transforms our outlook on life so that we live more fully in the present, welcome the future and have many feel good memories from the past.

Full transformation is when we have fully integrated this into our daily life and it all happens automatically. We never know how wonderful life can be until we get there. Often it is beyond our present comprehension or our wildest dreams.

Perception is based on the build-up of verbal and non-verbal suggestions that we have gathered throughout our life experience. It is through patterns of experimentation and repetition linked to the related feel good or feel bad results that we learn to create our own perception of reality.

High energy thoughts, actions and emotions, boost the immune system, and are vital for producing feel good results. Low energy thoughts, actions and emotions actually do the opposite.

NO. 3
OBJECTIVE REALITY

By practising Sophro-ki® Sophrology we will learn to leave the world of habitual interpretation. We learn to be conscious of what we are thinking and feeling in the moment and see things as much as possible as they really are, not as we think they are.

We accept our reality and the reality around us and others as they are, without judgment. It is as if we see things for the first time without labelling.

To be objective means not labelling what is happening with preconceptions, feelings, filters, beliefs, attitudes and ideas from the similar situations in the past. It means being fully present with heightened senses.

Instead of putting our past experiences in front of us and expecting the future to be similar we view what is happening as if it is the first time it has ever happened and be open to new possibilities and new outcomes.

An example could be that we phone somebody and they are very unpleasant and unhelpful. Three weeks later we need to phone that person for some more information.

We have a choice, we can assume that they are going to be the same as before and, if we do, we probably put off phoning as long as possible or try to find out the information in another way or even ask somebody else to phone.

If on the other hand we take the phenomenological approach, we would put our previous experience behind us and be open to new possibilities.

So instead of sending 'I know you are going to be a problem vibrations to the other person, we send, neutral open vibrations allowing them to be whoever they are today'.

Perhaps the person reacts in a similar way to before, however, by being neutral and open we are much less affected by their heavy emotions.

Objective reality is developed through regular Sophro-ki® Sophrology practice. We start to observe what we are thinking and feeling from an objective viewpoint.

By observing our thoughts objectively, we begin to stop identifying with them. Realising that our opinions of right or wrong, good or bad are from our conditioned mind and that there could, in fact, many more ways of viewing a situation.

Sometimes we are so trapped in thoughts of the future or the past, that we forget to experience or enjoy, what's happening right now!.

Objective reality takes us deeper into the truth of being, to a place of serenity, where we are at one with our self and everything else around us.

3 Fundamental Principles of Sophro-ki© Sophrology

WHAT HAPPENS IN A SOPHRO-KI®
SOPHROLOGY EXERCISE?

We do exercises sitting, standing and walking. This means that there is a Sophro-ki® Sophrology exercise that you can do wherever you are and whenever you have a few spare moments.

While on the train to work, in the office, while standing at the checkout in the supermarket, while waiting for a meeting to start, while walking in nature, at home, in bed, on the beach, anytime, anywhere…

It is important to know that there are 3 main parts to every Sophro-ki® Sophrology exercise. These parts can be shortened or lengthened to construct a Sophro-ki® Sophrology exercise of anything from 3mins to 45mins.

In between each part there is a Sophro Integration Pause. This is the most important part of the exercise. During this pause we focus on the body, noticing all the physical sensations (warm/cold, heavy/light, tingling/not tingling, tension/relaxation, etc.).

The many benefits of the Integration pause include:

- You develop concentration

- You experience being in present time

- You feel which parts of your body are tense or relaxed

- Your body realizes it is being listened to

- You become more aware of the body

- You notice where and how the body expresses each emotion

- You can make better decisions

- Your physical and mental health improves

- The list is long…

If you like you could try adding sophro integration pauses to your daily life. Just stopping for a few seconds and noticing what is happening, 'right now' in your body can make significant positive changes to your life.

 First Part

Consists of a body scan, tension release and breathing in energy into the cells. Sometimes the sophrologist will use all of these and sometimes just one or two. Typically there is always a body scan.

 Second part

The specific topic of each exercise e.g. relaxing physical and/or mental exercise.

 Third part

Activating 3 of our capacities, thereafter, stretching moving and opening the eyes, with Sophro Integration Pauses throughout the exercise

You could perhaps imagine a Sophro-ki® Sophrology exercise much like a sandwich – the bread is similar each time on either side but in the middle there is a different filling each time.

Once the exercise has finished and your eyes are open we recommend that you write up the experience in your sophro journal.

What types of things would you write in your journal?

Well anything that you remember, that you became aware of, that you want to recall, – it could be changes in temperature, body sensations, including their location, size, shape, and colour in the body, or most anything, it is your unique experience and it is your body.

6 TIPS TO HELP YOU GET THE MOST OUT OF EACH EXERCISE

1. Listen to the Introduction for information on how to do the exercise.

2. Put aside all previous knowledge, beliefs and attitudes.

3. Do the exercise 'as if it is the first time' free from judgment.

4. Be full of curiosity and wonder.

5. After the exercise take a moment to write down the feelings and sensations you experienced while listening.

6. Do each exercise daily for at least one week or more.

WHO DOES SOPHRO-KI® SOPHROLOGY?

SPORT

Pro Golfer, Sergio Garcia, has openly sung the praises of Sophro-ki® Sophrology. The improvement in his game, he says, is thanks to the regular practice of Sophro-ki® Sophrology.

The Swiss Clay Pigeon Shooting champions were trained by Energy Centre for the European Championships.

Tennis player – André Agassi did Sophro-ki® Sophrology for mind focus and concentration.

GENEVA SECONDARY SCHOOLS

Dorna Revie is employed by the Department of Education to give Sophro-ki® Sophrology workshops, entitled, "Dynamiser la vie scolaire et réussir les examens." in the Secondary Schools. "Enjoy school life and succeed in exams."

COMPANIES AND ORGANISATIONS

Companies who offer Sophro-ki® Sophrology training to their staff see a measurable reduction in absenteeism and a marked increase in motivation and efficiency.

ONE-2-ONE

Sophro One-2-One is like a holistic coaching programme in which clients let go of their limitations, fears, phobias and unhelpful habits and learn how to actively create the life that they dream of having.

PREGNANT WOMEN

Widely used in France, Switzerland, Japan and Korea for childbirth preparation and for post natal support.

HOSPITALS

Used by many hospitals to prepare patients for MRI scans, operation, chemotherapy and any potentially stressful intervention.

CAN I DO SOPHRO-KI® SOPHROLOGY ONLINE?

Since our aim is to reach out to as many people as possible, we have developed an online training program, you can download these from our website: www.sophrologycenteronline.com

MEET THE TEAM

We invite you to share this eBook with the people in your life who you feel would benefit from practising Sophro-ki® Sophrology.

Diana Ritchie
Sophrologist, trained at Energy Centre and Co-creator of SophroSunday

Michele Stohen
Communications and Social Media Director, Energy Centre

Darja Jovanovic
Client Care and Operations Manager, Energy Centre

To find out more and to download Sophro-ki® Sophrology exercises please visit us at: www.sophrologycenteronline.com

10757802R00026

Printed in Great Britain
by Amazon